the

RESCUE

project

STORY GUIDE
for participants
REVISED EDITION

ACTS

Know the Story
The Rescue Project *Story Guide*
Revised Edition
ACTS XXIX, Copyright © 2023. All rights reserved.

Layout by Jacqueline L. Challiss Hill ~ JDetailsLLC.com

Cover Image: ACTS XXIX
Image Credits: 4PM Media

https://rescueproject.us

Synopsis: The Story Guide is a companion resource for The Rescue Project that equips participants to engage in small group discussion over the eight week sessions.

ISBN: 978-1-7364920-6-2
Library of Congress Control Number: 2023903880

Printed in The United States of America

Published by ACTS XXIX Press
38695 Seven Mile Road, Suite 110
Livonia, MI 48152
actsxxix.org | press@actsxxix.org

Table of Contents

worldview

Chapter One

The Importance of Stories

"This is how stories work. They invite listeners into a new world and encourage them to make it their own, to see their ordinary world from now on through this lens, within this grid." [1]

- N.T. Wright,
Jesus and the Victory of God

For I am not ashamed of the gospel, for it is the power of God for salvation...

Romans 1:16

THEMES

The Four Big Questions

- Why is there something, rather than nothing?
- Why is everything so messed up?
- What, if anything, has God done about it?
- And if he's done anything, how should I respond?

QUESTIONS TO CONSIDER

- What is the story that gives me meaning, purpose, and guides my life?
- What is my image of God?
- Where did that image of God come from?

_____

_____

_____

_____

_____

_____

_____

_____

_____

_____

_____

_____

_____

_____

_____

_____

_____

SUGGESTED READING

Sophia Consulting. *Christian Cosmic Narrative: The Deep History of the World*, 2021.

Riccardo, Fr. John. *Rescued: The Unexpected and Extraordinary News of the Gospel*, 2020.

---

1. Wright, *Jesus and the Victory of God*, 176.

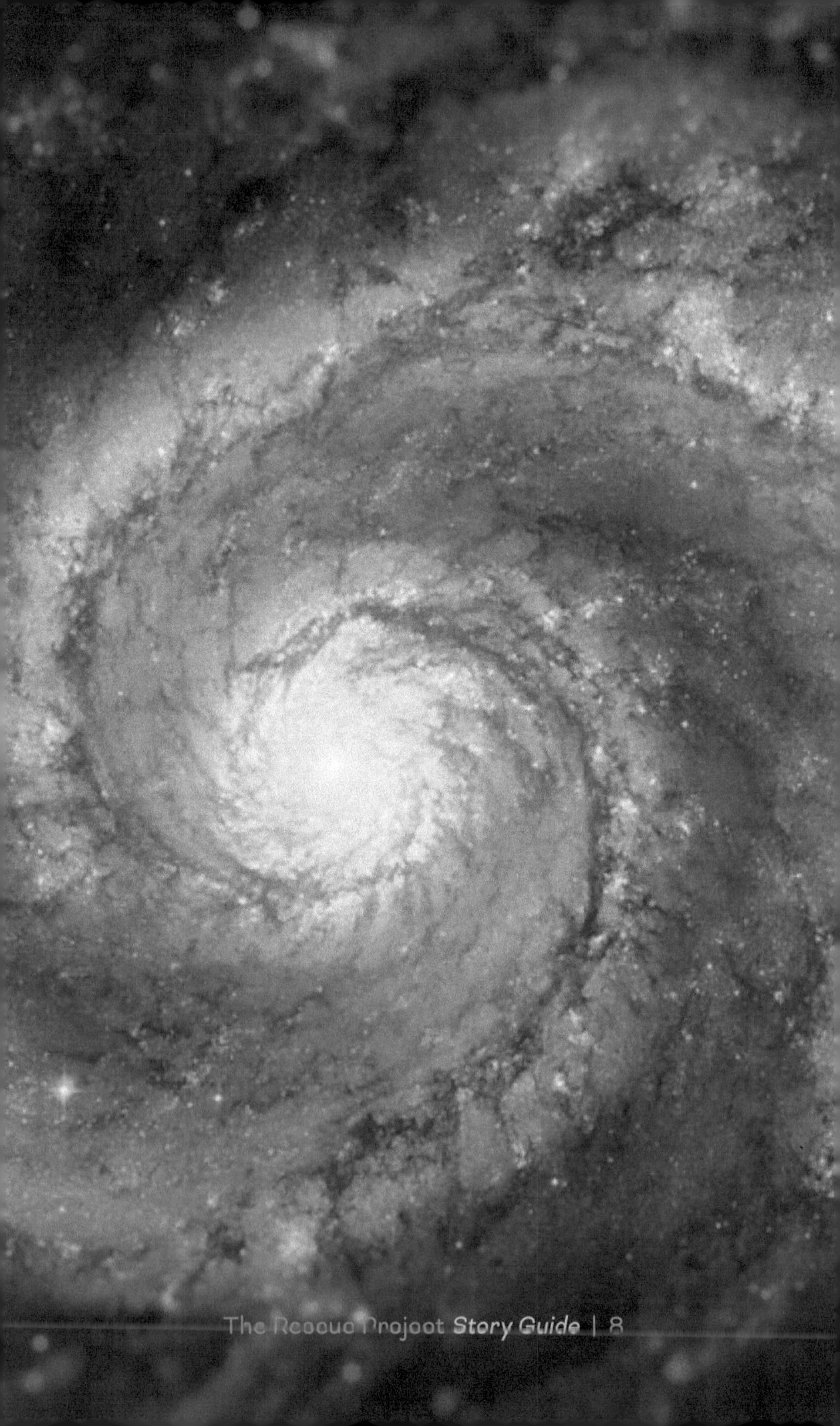

Chapter Two

Why Is There Something Rather than Nothing?

"Either all individual things are the product of evolution, including man, or else they are not... Of course, the question remains open whether being ... has a meaning and it cannot be decided within the theory of evolution itself; for that theory this is a methodologically foreign question, although of course for a live human being it is the fundamental question on which the whole thing depends." [2]

- Joseph Ratzinger,
Credo for Today: What Christians Believe

THE GRACE: *Wonder and Awe*

And God made the two great lights, the greater light to rule the day and the lesser light to rule the night; he made the stars also.[3]

Genesis 1:16

THEMES

The Biblical Story

- There is one God.
- He is good.
- He creates out of love (and not need).
- He creates effortlessly.
- The human person is the highlight of everything that he creates.
- We are made in his image and likeness.
- We are made for friendship, love, and communion with God and with each other.

QUESTIONS TO CONSIDER

- How does pondering the grandeur of creation instill a sense of wonder and awe in my life?
  How or why?
- Is my image of God changing? Yes or No? Explain.
- What's causing me anxiety right now? How does the God of the biblical story impact that?

_____

_____

_____

_____

_____

_____

_____

_____

_____

_____

RESOURCES

Catechism of the Catholic Church 295-301:
"The Mystery of Creation"

295 We believe that God created the world according to his wisdom. It is not the product of any necessity whatever, nor of blind fate or chance. We believe that it proceeds from God's free will; he wanted to make his creatures share in his being, wisdom and goodness: "For you created all things, and by your will they existed and were created." Therefore, the Psalmist exclaims: "O LORD, how manifold are your works! In wisdom you have made them all"; and "The LORD is good to all, and his compassion is over all that he has made."

God creates "out of nothing"

296 We believe that God needs no pre-existent thing or any help in order to create, nor is creation any sort of necessary emanation from the divine substance. God creates freely "out of nothing":

If God had drawn the world from pre-existent matter, what would be so extraordinary in that?

A human artisan makes from a given material whatever he wants, while God shows his power by starting from nothing to make all he wants.

297 Scripture bears witness to faith in creation "out of nothing" as a truth full of promise and hope. Thus, the mother of seven sons encourages them for martyrdom:

I do not know how you came into being in my womb. It was not I who gave you life and breath, nor I who set in order the elements within each of you. Therefore, the Creator of the world, who shaped the beginning of man and devised the origin of all things, will in his mercy give life and breath back to you again, since you now forget yourselves for the sake of his laws... Look at the heaven and the earth and see everything that is in them, and recognize that God did not make them out of things that existed. Thus, also mankind comes into being.

298 Since God could create everything out of nothing, he can also, through the Holy Spirit, give spiritual life to sinners by creating a pure heart in them, and bodily life to the dead through the Resurrection. God "gives life to the dead and calls into existence the things that do not exist" and since God was able to make light shine in darkness by his Word, he can also give the light of faith to those who do not yet know him.

God creates an ordered and good world

299 Because God creates through wisdom, his creation is ordered: "You have arranged all things by measure and number and weight." The universe, created in and by the eternal Word, the "image of the invisible God," is destined for and addressed to man, himself created in the "image of God" and called to a personal relationship

with God. Our human understanding, which shares in the light of the divine intellect, can understand what God tells us by means of his creation, though not without great effort and only in a spirit of humility and respect before the Creator and his work. Because creation comes forth from God's goodness, it shares in that goodness– "and God saw that it was good… very good"– for God willed creation as a gift addressed to man, an inheritance destined for and entrusted to him. On many occasions the Church has had to defend the goodness of creation, including that of the physical world.

God transcends creation and is present to it

300 God is infinitely greater than all his works: "You have set your glory above the heavens." Indeed, God's "greatness is unsearchable." But because he is the free and sovereign Creator, the first cause of all that exists, God is present to his creatures' inmost being: "In him we live and move and have our being." In the words of St. Augustine, God is "higher than my highest and more inward than my innermost self."

God upholds and sustains creation

301 With creation, God does not abandon his creatures to themselves. He not only gives them being and existence, but also, and at every moment, upholds and sustains them in being, enables them to act and brings them to their final end. Recognizing this utter dependence with respect to the Creator is a source of wisdom and freedom, of joy and confidence:

For you love all things that exist, and detest none of the things that you have made; for you would not have made anything if you had hated it. How would anything have endured, if you had not willed it? Or how would anything not called forth by you have been preserved? You spare all things, for they are yours, O Lord, you who love the living.[4]

SUGGESTED READING

Johnston, George. "How to Read the First Chapters of Genesis." *Lay Witness,* 1998.

Kreeft, Peter. *You Can Understand the Bible,* 2005.

Documents of Vatican II. "Dogmatic Constitution on Divine Revelation." *Dei Verbum,* 1965.

Pope Benedict XVI. *"In the Beginning...": A Catholic Understanding of the Story of Creation and the Fall,* 2013.

---

2. Ratzinger, *Credo for Today: What Christians Believe,* 37.
3. Gen. 1:16 RSV.
4. *Catechism of the Catholic Church,* 295-301: "The Mystery of Creation".

Chapter Three

The Enemy Is the Enemy

"The sight of these happy creatures filled the devil and his fallen angels with anger and envy. They took thought as to how they might mar the work of God and destroy the destiny of this newly created race. They set about to enslave those whom they had been meant to serve and to degrade those who had been assigned such an exalted place into the lowly slime beneath their feet." [5]

- Sophia Consulting,
The Christian Cosmic Narrative

THE GRACE: *Light*

But by the envy of the devil, Death entered the world, and those who are in his possession experience it.[6]

Wisdom 2:24

THEMES

The Enemy: Five Key Questions
• Who is he?
• Why did he rebel?
• What's his lie?
• What are his tactics?
• What's his goal for my life?

QUESTIONS TO CONSIDER

- Where is the enemy accusing me right now?
- What lie is crippling me right now?
- Where is the enemy causing division in my life right now?
- Where is the enemy flattering my ego right now?
- What temptation is strongest in my life right now?
- Where am I most discouraged right now?

_____

_____

_____

_____

_____

_____

_____

_____

_____

_____

RESOURCES

Catechism of the Catholic Church 391-395:
"The Fall of the Angels"

391 Behind the disobedient choice of our first parents lurks a seductive voice, opposed to God, which makes them fall into death out of envy. Scripture and the Church's Tradition see in this being a fallen angel, called "Satan" or the "devil." The Church teaches that Satan was at first a good angel, made by God: "The devil and the other demons were indeed created naturally good by God, but they became evil by their own doing."

392 Scripture speaks of a sin of these angels. This "fall" consists in the free choice of these created spirits, who radically and irrevocably rejected God and his reign. We find a reflection of that rebellion in the tempter's words to our first parents: "You will be like God." The devil "has sinned from the beginning"; he is "a liar and the father of lies."

393 It is the *irrevocable* character of their choice, and not a defect in the infinite divine mercy, that makes the angels' sin unforgivable. "There is no repentance for the angels after their fall, just as there is no repentance for men after death."

394 Scripture witnesses to the disastrous influence of the one Jesus calls "a murderer from the beginning," who would even try to divert Jesus from the mission received from his Father. "The reason the Son of God appeared was to destroy the works of the devil." In its consequences the gravest of these works was the mendacious seduction that led man to disobey God.

395 The power of Satan is, nonetheless, not infinite. He is only a creature, powerful from the fact that he is pure spirit, but still a creature. He cannot prevent the building up of God's reign. Although Satan may act in the world out of hatred for God and his kingdom in Christ Jesus, and although his action may cause grave injuries–of a spiritual nature and, indirectly, even of a physical nature–to each man and to society, the action is permitted by divine providence which with strength and gentleness guides human and cosmic history. It is a great mystery that providence should permit diabolical activity, but "we know that in everything God works for good with those who love him." [7]

SUGGESTED READING

Lewis, C. S. *The Screwtape Letters,* 1942.

Spitzer, Fr. Robert. *Christ and Satan in Our Daily Lives,* 2020.

---

5. Sophia Consulting, *The Christian Cosmic Narrative,* 23.
6. *Lectionary for Mass,* 2002, Wisdom 2:24.
7. *Catechism of the Catholic Church* 391-395: "The Fall of the Angels."

Chapter Four

It Gets Worse

"The controlling metaphor of this section is slavery and freedom. Paul paints a black-or-white picture of the human situation: either one lives in service to sin and remains in spiritual bondage, or one lives in obedience to God and enjoys liberation from sin's captivity. It is a stark either-or: no fence-sitting, no third option." [8]

- Dr. Scott Hahn,
Commentary on Romans

THE GRACE: *Despair*

When a strongman, fully armed, guards his own palace, his goods are safe; but when one stronger than he attacks him and overcomes him, he takes away his armor in which he trusted and divides his spoil.

Luke 11:21-22

THEMES

The Strongman Parable
- The strongman – *the enemy*
- His palace – *the world*
- His goods – *humankind*
- The stronger one – *Jesus*

QUESTIONS TO CONSIDER

- What am I thinking and feeling right now?
- Did God reveal something new to me about how the enemy works in my life?
- How does the Biblical Story's vision that the enemy is the enemy (and that he divides and accuses) change the way I think about what is happening around me right now?

_____

_____

_____

_____

_____

_____

_____

_____

_____

RESOURCES

Catechism of the Catholic Church 396-401:
"Original Sin"

Freedom put to the test

396 God created man in his image and established him in his friendship. A spiritual creature, man can live this friendship only in free submission to God. The prohibition against eating "of the tree of the knowledge of good and evil" spells this out: "for in the day that you eat of it, you shall die." The "tree of the knowledge of good and evil" symbolically evokes the insurmountable limits that man, being a creature, must freely recognize and respect with trust. Man is dependent on his Creator, and subject to the laws of creation and to the moral norms that govern the use of freedom.

Man's first sin

397 Man, tempted by the devil, let his trust in his Creator die in his heart and, abusing his freedom, disobeyed God's command. This is what man's first sin consisted of. All subsequent sin would be disobedience toward God and lack of trust in his goodness.

398 In that sin man *preferred* himself to God and by that very act scorned him. He chose himself over and

against God, against the requirements of his creaturely status and therefore against his own good. Created in a state of holiness, man was destined to be fully "divinized" by God in glory. Seduced by the devil, he wanted to "be like God," but "without God, before God, and not in accordance with God."

399 Scripture portrays the tragic consequences of this first disobedience. Adam and Eve immediately lose the grace of original holiness. They become afraid of the God of whom they have conceived a distorted image–that of a God jealous of his prerogatives.

400 The harmony in which they had found themselves, thanks to original justice, is now destroyed: the control of the soul's spiritual faculties over the body is shattered; the union of man and woman becomes subject to tensions, their relations henceforth marked by lust and domination. Harmony with creation is broken: visible creation has become alien and hostile to man. Because of man, creation is now subject "to its bondage to decay." Finally, the consequence explicitly foretold for this disobedience will come true: man will "return to the ground," for out of it he was taken.

Death makes its entrance into human history

401 After that first sin, the world is virtually inundated by sin. There is Cain's murder of his brother Abel and the universal corruption which follows in the wake of sin. Likewise, sin frequently manifests itself in the history of Israel, especially as infidelity to the God of the

Covenant and as transgression of the Law of Moses. And even after Christ's atonement, sin raises its head in countless ways among Christians. Scripture and the Church's Tradition continually recall the presence and *universality of sin in man's history:*

What Revelation makes known to us is confirmed by our own experience. For when man looks into his own heart he finds that he is drawn towards what is wrong and sunk in many evils which cannot come from his good creator. Often refusing to acknowledge God as his source, man has also upset the relationship which should link him to his last end, and at the same time he has broken the right order that should reign within himself as well as between himself and other men and all creatures. [9]

SUGGESTED READING

Rutledge, Fleming. *The Crucifixion: Understanding the Death of Jesus,* 2015.

---

8. Hahn, *Commentary on Romans,* 102.

9. *Catechism of the Catholic Church* 396-401: "Original Sin."

Chapter Five

Why Did Jesus Come?

"Lord God Almighty, who sent Your Only Begotten Son to endow humankind, imprisoned in slavery to Sin, with the freedom of Your sons and daughters, we pray most humbly for these children, whom You know will experience the allurements of this world, and will fight against the snares of the devil: by the power of the Passion and Resurrection of Your Son deliver them now from the stain of Original Sin, strengthen them with the grace of Christ, and guard them always on their journey through life." [10]

- Baptismal Ritual of the Catholic Church

THE GRACE: *Light*

For thus says the Lord:
"Even the captives of the mighty shall be taken, and the prey of the tyrant be rescued, for I will contend with those who contend with you, and I will save your children. . . .Then all flesh shall know that I am the Lord your Savior, and your Redeemer, the Mighty One of Jacob."

Isaiah 49:25-26

THEMES

What was Jesus *doing* on the cross?
1. Showing us the love of the Father.
2. Making atonement; becoming Sin.
3. Going to war to rescue us.

QUESTIONS TO CONSIDER

- What am I thinking and how am I feeling now?
- How does the story of Jesus as a warrior coming to rescue me change how I see him?
- Does understanding that Jesus didn't only do this for me change how I see and treat others?

_____

_____

_____

_____

_____

_____

_____

_____

_____

_____

_____

RESOURCES

The Greatest Philosopher Who Ever Lived, Peter Kreeft.

"The first question a child asks about a story is: What is it about? Is it a love story, a war story, an adventure story, a psychological drama, or what? The question presupposes that there is an answer to it and that the author of the story knows the answer, that he is in charge, that he knows what kind of story he is telling...

"In one sense, the story of human history is a love story. But in a fallen world, a love story is always also a war story. In fact, the single fundamental theme of every story since the Fall has always been the war between good and evil. That is the theme of the Bible, especially in the last book, Revelation, which symbolically summarizes and interprets all the little stories in terms of the big story...

"God Himself announces this theme, within the story itself. For this God, unlike the God of deism, reveals Himself to us. In fact, he makes himself a character in the story as well as being the transcendent Author of it...

"Immediately after the Fall, which is the beginning of human history, he announces the theme of his story, of history. It is war: 'I will put enmity [war] between you [Satan] and the Woman [Eve]...'

"This is the first Gospel, the 'proto-evangelium.' Strange as it sounds, the Gospel is a war story. No one can read the four Gospels alertly and intelligently and open-mindedly without seeing that. The 'liberal' point that Jesus was simply to teach love is about as accurate as the idea that the purpose of Adolf Hitler was to create world peace. For in a fallen world, the only way that there can be love is for there to be war. Love wars. Love fights. Ask any mother, in any species of mammal, especially homo sapiens.

"Christ versus Antichrist, the City of God versus the City of This World, the Holy Spirit and His angels versus the Devil and his fallen angels, light versus darkness, good versus evil - that is the plot...

"The warfare, of course, is spiritual in its root and in its essence. 'We are not contending against flesh and blood, but against the principalities, against the powers, against the world rulers of this present darkness' (Eph. 6:12)." [11]

Selected Writings of the Early Church Fathers on the Paschal Mystery

St. Ignatius of Antioch *(c. 50-110)*
There was concealed from the ruler of this world the virginity of Mary and the birth of our Lord, and the three renowned mysteries which were done in the tranquility of God from the star. And here, at the manifestation of the Son, magic began to be destroyed, and all bonds were loosed; and the ancient kingdom and the error

of evil was destroyed. Henceforward all things were moved together, and the destruction of death was devised, and there was the commencement of that which was perfected in God. [12]

St. Justin Martyr (c. 100-165)

Christ became man by the Virgin, in order that the disobedience that proceeded from the serpent might receive its destruction in the same manner in which it derived its origin. For Eve, who was a virgin and undefiled, having conceived the word of the serpent, brought forth disobedience and death. But the Virgin Mary received faith and joy when the angel Gabriel announced the good tidings to her that the Spirit of the Lord would come upon her, and the power of the Highest would overshadow her: wherefore also the Holy Thing begotten of her is the Son of God; and she replied, "Be it unto me according to Thy word" (Lk 1:38). And by her has He been born, to Whom we have proved so many Scriptures refer, and by Whom God destroys both the serpent and those angels and men who are like him. [13]

St. Melito of Sardis (c. 120-185)

Who is he who contends with Me? Let him stand in opposition to Me. I set the condemned man free; I gave the dead man life; I raised up the one who had been entombed. Who is My opponent? I, He says, am the Christ. I am the One who destroyed death, and triumphed over the enemy, and trampled Hades under foot, and bound the strong one, and carried off man to the heights of heaven. I, he says, am the Christ. This is the alpha and the omega. This is the beginning and the end—an indescribable beginning and an incomprehensible end. This is the Christ. This is the King. This is Jesus. This is the General. This is the Lord. This is the One who rose up from the dead. This is the One who sits at the right hand of the Father. [14]

———————

St. Irenaeus (c. 130-202)
Let us, then, put the question again: For what purpose did Christ come down from heaven?

Answer: "That He might destroy sin, overcome death, and give life to man." By the side of this pregnant saying we will set another, chosen from among many similar passages, which develops the dramatic idea in fuller detail: "Man had been created by God that he might have life. If now, having lost life, and having been harmed by the serpent, he were not to return to life, but were to be wholly abandoned to death, then God would have been defeated, and the malice of the serpent would have overcome God's will. But since God is both invincible and magnanimous, he showed his magnanimity in correcting man, and in proving all men, as we have said; but through the Second Man he bound the strong one, and spoiled his goods, and annihilated death, bringing life to man who had become subject to death. For Adam had become the devil's possession, and the devil held him under his power, by having wrongfully practiced deceit upon him, and by the offer of immortality made him subject to death. For by promising that they should be as gods, which did not lie in his power, he worked death in them. Wherefore he who had taken man captive was himself taken captive by God, and man who had been taken captive was set free from the bondage of condemnation."

"The Word of God," he says, "was made flesh in order that He might destroy death and bring man to life; for we were tied and bound in sin, we were born in sin and live under the dominion of death." [15]

St. Gregory of Nyssa (c. 335-395)
He was about to engage him who had taken human nature prisoner and was about to loosen death's bonds; by having destroyed the last enemy [cf. 1 Cor. 15:26], he might restore mankind to freedom and peace.

In order to secure that the ransom in our behalf might be easily accepted by him who required it, the Deity was hidden under the veil of our nature, that so, as with ravenous fish, the hook of the Deity might be gulped down along with the bait of flesh, and thus, life being introduced into the house of death, and light shining in darkness, that which is diametrically opposed to light and life might vanish; for it is not in the nature of darkness to remain when light is present, or of death to exist when life is active. [16]

The devil jumped for joy when Christ died; and by the very death of Christ the devil was overcome: he took, as it were, the bait in the mousetrap. He rejoiced at the death, thinking himself death's commander. But that which caused his joy dangled the bait before him. The Lord's cross was the devil's mousetrap: the bait which caught him was the death of the Lord.

The next verse explains something of the reason why so much honor should be paid to him, and why all nations should serve him: He has delivered the needy from the tyrant, that poor person who had no other champion. This needy and poor person is the people that believes in him, and within this people are kings who worship him. They are not too proud to be needy and poor, which means humbly acknowledging that they are sinners and in need of the glory of God, so that the true King, the Son of the King, may free them from the powerful foe. Powerful indeed he is who has been called the accuser. Yet it was not his own strength that brought men and women into subjection to this powerful tyrant, and kept them there in captivity, but human sins. The powerful tyrant is also called in scripture "the strong man," but Christ, who humiliated the accuser, also broke into the strong man's domain to bind him and seize his possessions. Christ is the one who has delivered the needy from the tyrant, that poor person who had no other champion, for no one else had the strength to accomplish that—no righteous person nor even any angel. There was no champion at all, therefore; but Christ came and saved them.

Having despoiled the devil, Christ distributes his gifts to beautify the Church. The psalm proceeds: It is the Beloved's part also to divide the spoils for the beauty of the house. The word Beloved is repeated for emphasis. But in fact it is not all the codices that have this repetition, and the more exact among them prefix a star to it. Such signs are called asterisks, and they inform us that the passages so marked are present in the Hebrew, but not in the interpretation by the Septuagint. But whether we think Beloved was repeated, or was written once only, I think we must take the words that follow it, to divide the spoils for the beauty of the house, in the sense, it is the Beloved's part also to divide the spoils for the beauty of the house; that is, he was chosen also for the division of the spoils. Undoubtedly the Church which Christ has created is a beautiful house, and he has adorned it by distributing his spoils to it, as a body is made beautiful by the due distribution of its limbs. Now the word "spoils" is used of goods seized from vanquished enemies, and the gospel throws light on this passage by saying, No one can get into a strong man's house and carry off his implements, unless he has tied up the strong man first (Mt. 12:29). Christ tied up the devil with spiritual chains by overcoming death and ascending from the underworld to heaven; he bound the devil by the sacrament of his incarnation, because although the devil found nothing in Christ that deserved death, he was nonetheless allowed to kill him. The consequence was that Christ tied up the devil and took away his belongings as booty. These were the unbelievers through whom the devil worked his will. But the Lord cleansed these tools by forgiving their sins; he left the enemy felled and chained, and sanctified the spoils he had seized. He then assigned them to their due places for the adornment of his own house, appointing some to be apostles, some prophets, some pastors and teachers for the work of ministry, for the building up of the body of Christ.

We are thy servants, we are thy creatures: Thou hast made us, thou hast redeemed us. Anyone can buy his servant, create him he cannot; but the Lord hath both created and redeemed his servants; created them, that they might be; redeemed them, that they might not be captives ever. For we fell into the hands of the prince of this world, who seduced Adam, and made him his servant, and began to possess us as his slaves. But the Redeemer came, and the seducer was overcome. And what did our Redeemer to him who held us captive? For our ransom he held out his cross as a trap; he placed in It as a bait his blood. He indeed had power to shed his blood, he did not attain to drink it. And in that he shed the blood of him who was no debtor, he was commanded to render up the debtors; he shed the blood of the Innocent, he was commanded to withdraw from the guilty. He verily shed his blood to this end, that he might wipe out our sins. That then whereby he held us fast was effaced by the Redeemer's blood. For he only held us fast by the bonds of our own sins. They were the captive's chains. He came, he bound the strong one with the bonds of his passion; He entered into his house, into the hearts, that is, of those where he did dwell, and took away his vessels. We are his vessels. He had filled then with his own bitterness. This bitterness too he pledged to our Redeemer in the gall. He had filled us then as his vessels; but our Lord spoiling his vessels, and making them his own, poured out the bitterness, filled them with sweetness. [17]

———

St. Ephrem (c. 306-373)

Death trampled our Lord underfoot, but he in his turn treated death as a highroad for his own feet. He submitted to it, enduring it willingly, because by this means he would be able to destroy death in spite of itself.

Death had its own way when our Lord went out from Jerusalem carrying his cross; but when by a loud cry from that cross he summoned the dead from the underworld, death was powerless to prevent it.

Death slew him by means of the body which he had assumed, but that same body proved to be the weapon with which he conquered death. Concealed beneath the cloak of his manhood, his godhead engaged death in combat; but in slaying our Lord, death itself was slain. It was able to kill natural human life, but was itself killed by the life that is above the nature of man.

Death could not devour our Lord unless he possessed a body, neither could hell swallow him up unless he bore our flesh; and so he came in search of a chariot in which to ride to the underworld. This chariot was the body which he received from the Virgin; in it he invaded death's fortress, broke open its strong-room and scattered all its treasure. [18]

———

St. John Chrysostom (c. 347-407)

Whosoever is pious and loves God, let him enjoy this good and cheerful festival. Whosoever is a grateful servant, let him rejoice and enter into the joy of the Lord. Whosoever is weary of fasting, let him now receive his earnings. Whosoever has laboured from the first hour, let him today accept his just reward. Whosoever has come after the third hour, let him with thanksgiving take part in the celebration. Whosoever has arrived after the sixth hour, let him have no misgivings, for he too shall suffer no loss. Whosoever has delayed until the ninth hour, let him approach without hesitation. Whosoever has arrived only at the eleventh hour, let him not fear the delay, for the Master is gracious: He receives the last even as the first; He gives rest to him that comes at the eleventh hour, as well as to him that has laboured from the first; and to him that delayed he gives mercy, and the first he restores to health; to the one he gives, to the other he bestows.

And he accepts the works, and embraces the contemplation; the deed he honours, and the intention he commends.

Therefore let everyone enter into the joy of the Lord. The first and the last, receive your wages. Rich and poor, dance with each other. The temperate and the slothful, honour this day. Ye who have fasted and ye who have not, rejoice this day. The table is fully laden; all of you delight in it. The calf is plenteous, let no one depart hungry. Let everyone enjoy this banquet of faith. Let everyone take pleasure in the wealth of goodness. Let no one lament his poverty, for the universal kingdom has appeared. Let no one bewail for his transgressions, for forgiveness has risen from the grave. Let no one fear death, for the Saviours death has set us free. He who was held by death, eradicated death. He plundered Hades when He descended into Hades. He embittered it, when it tasted of his flesh, and this being foretold by Isaiah when he cried: Hades said it was embittered, when it encountered Thee below. Embittered, for it was abolished. Embittered, for it was ridiculed. Embittered, for it was put to death. Embittered, for it was dethroned. Embittered, for it was made captive.

It received a body and by chance came face to face with God. It received earth and encountered heaven. It received that which it could see, and was overthrown by him whom he could not see. Where, O death, is your sting? Where, O Hades, is your victory? Christ is risen, and thou art cast down. Christ is risen, and the demons have fallen. Christ is risen, and the angels rejoice. Christ is risen, and life is liberated. Christ is risen, and no one remains dead in a tomb. For Christ having risen from the dead, has become the first-fruits of those that have fallen asleep. To him be glory and power, for ever and ever.
Amen. [19]

———————

St. Leo the Great (c. 400-461)
When, therefore, the merciful and almighty Saviour so arranged the commencement of His human course as to hide the power of his Godhead which was insepara-

ble from his manhood under the veil of our weakness, the crafty foe was taken off his guard and he thought that the nativity of the child, who was born for the salvation of mankind, was as much subject to himself as all others are at their birth. For he saw him crying and weeping, he saw him wrapped in swaddling clothes, subjected to circumcision, offering the sacrifice which the law required. And then he perceived in him the usual growth of boyhood, and could have had no doubt of His reaching man's estate by natural steps.

Meanwhile, he inflicted insults, multiplied injuries, made use of curses, affronts, blasphemies, abuse, in a word, poured upon him all the force of his fury and exhausted all the varieties of trial: and knowing how he had poisoned man's nature, had no conception that he had no share in the first transgression whose mortality he had ascertained by so many proofs. The unscrupulous thief and greedy robber persisted in assaulting Him Who had nothing of his own, and in carrying out the general sentence on original sin, went beyond the bond on which he rested, and required the punishment of iniquity from him in whom he found no fault. And thus the malevolent terms of the deadly compact are annulled, and through the injustice of an overcharge the whole debt is cancelled. The strong one is bound by his own chains, and every device of the evil one recoils on his own head. When the prince of the world is bound, all that he held in captivity is released. Our nature cleansed from its old contagion regains its honourable estate, death is destroyed by death, nativity is restored by nativity: since at one and the same time redemption does away with

slavery, regeneration changes our origin, and faith jus-
tifies the sinner. [20]

The Council of Chalcedon (451)

His birth in time in no way subtracts from or adds to that
divine and eternal birth of his: but its whole purpose is
to restore humanity, who had been deceived, so that it
might defeat death and, by its power, destroy the devil
who held the power of death. Overcoming the originator
of sin and death would be beyond us, had not he whom
sin could not defile, nor could death hold down, taken up
our nature and made it his own. He was conceived from
the Holy Spirit inside the womb of the virgin mother.
Her virginity was as untouched in giving him birth as it
was in conceiving him. [21]

St. Isidore of Seville (c. 560-636)

The devil was deluded by the death of the Lord... for
through the visible mortality of his flesh, Christ—whom
the devil was trying to kill—concealed his divinity, like
a snare in which he might entangle him like an unwise
bird by a clever trick...The devil, although he attacked
the flesh of the humanity in Christ that was evident, was
captured as if by the fishhook of his divinity that was ly-
ing hidden. For there is in Christ the fishhook of divinity;
the food, however, is the flesh; the fishing line is the ge-
nealogy that is recited by the Gospel. Holding this fishing line truly is God the Father. [22]

St. Maximus the Confessor (c. 580-662)

His flesh was set before that voracious, gaping dragon as bait to provoke him: flesh that would be deadly for the dragon, for it would utterly destroy him by the power of the Godhead hidden within it. For human nature, however, his flesh was to be a remedy since the power of the Godhead in it would restore human nature to its original grace.

Just as the devil had poisoned the tree of knowledge and spoiled our nature by its taste, so too, in presuming to devour the Lord's flesh he himself is corrupted and is completely destroyed by the power of the Godhead hidden in it. [23]

St. Bernard (c. 1090-1153)

He comes as an Infant, and without speech, for the voice of the wailing infant arouses compassion, not terror. If He is terrible to any, yet not to thee. He is become a Little One, his Virgin Mother swathes His tender limbs with bands, and dost thou still tremble with fear? By this weakness thou mayest know that He comes not to destroy, but to save; not to bind, but to unbind. If He shall take up the sword, it will be against thine enemies, and, as the Power and the Wisdom of God, He will trample on the necks of the proud and the mighty. We have two enemies, sin and death—that is, the death of the soul and the death of the body. Jesus comes to conquer both, and to save us from both. Already he has vanquished sin in his own person by assuming a human nature free from the corruption of sin. For great violence was offered to sin, and it knew itself to be indeed subdued, when that nature which it gloried to have wholly infected and possessed was found in Christ perfectly free from its dominion. Henceforth Christ will pursue our enemies, and will seize them, and will not desist until they are overcome in us. His whole mortal life was a war against sin. He fought against it by word and example. But it was in his passion that he came upon the strong man armed, and bound him, and bore away his spoils.

Jesus Christ also conquers our second enemy, death. He overcomes it first in himself, when he rises from the dead, the first-fruits of them that sleep, and the first-born from the dead. Afterwards he will, in like manner, vanquish death in all of us when He shall raise our mortal bodies from the dust, and destroy this our last enemy. Thus, when he rose from the dead, Jesus was clothed in beauty, not wrapped in swaddling-clothes as at his birth. He that previously overflowed with mercy, "judging no man," girded himself in His resurrection with the girdle of justice, and in so doing seemed in some degree to restrain His superabundant mercy in order to be thenceforth prepared for the judgment which is to follow our future resurrection. [24]

St. Bonaventure (c. 1221-1274)
Now that the combat of the passion was over, and the bloody dragon and raging lion thought that he had secured a victory by killing the Lamb, the power of the divinity began to shine forth in his soul as it descended into hell. By this power our strong Lion of the tribe of

Judah (Apoc. 5:5), rising against the strong man who was fully armed (Luke 11:21), tore the prey away from him, broke down the gates of hell and bound the serpent. Disarming the Principalities and Powers, he led them away boldly, displaying them openly in triumph in himself (Col. 2:15). Then the Leviathan was led about with a hook (Job 40:25), his jaw pierced by Christ so that he who had no right over the Head which he had attacked, also lost what he had seemed to have over the body. Then the true Samson, as he died, laid prostrate an army of the enemy (cf. Judges 16:30). Then the Lamb without stain by the blood of his Testament led forth the prisoners from the pit in which there was no water (Zach. 9:11).

Then the long-awaited brightness of a new light shone upon those that dwelt in the region of the shadow of death (Isa. 9:2). [25]

QUESTION:

Did the devil know who Jesus was?

This often causes confusion, as it appears as though he does. Comments in the Gospels like, "We know who you are, the holy one of God," or "If you are the Son of God," seem to indicate that the devil and or the demons knew him. But this is not true. For one thing, love and humility are literally beyond hell's way of thinking, and God becoming flesh in the person of Jesus is the utmost in love and humility. Too, expressions like "holy one of God" or "Son of God" were common ways among the Jewish people of referring to the Messiah, who was not at all expected to be a divine person but rather a man.

Frank Sheed, in his book *To Know Christ Jesus,* puts it this way: "I think it was of the first urgency to find out what 'son of God' meant. It had been used in the Old Testament as a name for the Messiah (Ps. 2:7).

But did he know what it *meant?* 'Son of God' had been variously used in the Old Testament–of the chosen people, for instance (Ex 4:22), and, in the plural, of the Jewish judges (Ps 81:6). Satan knew his Old Testament, but the book of Job he must have scrutinized for special closeness, for so much of it was about a certain Satan and the high carnival he had at Job's expense. In that book (1:6, 2:1, 38:7) 'sons of God' meant the unfallen angels. Satan may well have weighed the possibility that the Messiah might be an angel, entering in some unforeseeable way into humanity for "the crushing of his head." [26]

10. *Baptismal Ritual of the Catholic Church*, 158.

11. Kreeft, *The Greatest Philosopher Who Ever Lived*, 247-248.

12. St. Ignatius of Antioch, "The Second Epistle of Ignatius to the Ephesians," 102.

13. St. Justin Martyr, "Dialogue with Trypho," 100.

14. St. Melito of Sardis, "Sermon on The Passover."

15. St. Irenaeus, *The Demonstration of the Apostolic Preaching*.

16. St. Gregory of Nyssa, *The Great Catechism*, ch. XXIV.

17. St. Augustine, "Expositions of the Psalms 51-72," 464-465.

18. St. Ephrem, "A Sermon on the Cross of Christ."

19. St. John Chrysostom, "The Easter Sermon of John Chrysostom."

20. St. Leo the Great, *"Sermon 22."*

21. The Council of Chalcedon. "The Letter of Pope Leo to Flavian."

22. Knoebel quoting Isidore of *Seville, Sententiae,* 61.

23. St. Maximus the Confessor, *Mystery of the Divine Incarnation*.

24. St. Bernard, "The Fountains of the Savior," *Sermons on Advent & Christmas,* 103-104.

25. St. Bonaventure, *The Soul's Journey to God,* 159.

26. Sheed, *To Know Christ Jesus,* 118.

Chapter Six

What Difference Does It Make?

"Let no one fear death, for the Death of our Savior has set us free. He has destroyed it by enduring it. He destroyed Hades when He descended into it. He put it into an uproar even as it tasted of His flesh. Isaiah foretold this when he said, 'You, O Hell, have been troubled by encountering Him below.' Hell was in an uproar because it was done away with. It was in an uproar because it is mocked. It was in an uproar, for it is destroyed. It is in an uproar, for it is annihilated. It is in an uproar, for it is now made captive. Hell took a body, and discovered God. It took earth, and encountered Heaven. It took what it saw, and was overcome by what it did not see. O death, where is thy sting? O Hades, where is thy victory?" [27]

- St. John Chrysostom

THE GRACE:
Unshakeable Confidence in Jesus

For he rescued us from the domain of Darkness, and transferred us to the kingdom of his beloved Son, in whom we have redemption, the forgiveness of sins. [28]

Colossians 1:13-14

THEMES

Jesus has...

· Humiliated the enemy.
· Transferred humanity from one dominion to another.
· Rendered Sin impotent.
· Destroyed the power of Death.
· Canceled our debt.
· Recreated us.
· Given us access to the Father.
· Given us authority over the enemy.
· Sent us on mission to get his world back.
· Divinized us.

QUESTIONS TO CONSIDER

- What am I thinking and how am I feeling right now?
- Which result of the resurrection of Jesus resonates most deeply with me and why?
- Calling to mind the importance of stories from Chapter One, what impact is the biblical story having on my life?

_____

_____

_____

_____

_____

_____

_____

_____

_____

_____

RESOURCES

Catechism of the Catholic Church 651-655: "The Meaning and Saving Significance of the Resurrection"

651 "If Christ has not been raised, then our preaching is in vain and your faith is in vain." The Resurrection above all constitutes the confirmation of all Christ's works and teachings. All truths, even those most inaccessible to human reason, find their justification if Christ by his Resurrection has given the definitive proof of his divine authority, which he had promised.

652 Christ's Resurrection is the fulfillment of the promises both of the Old Testament and of Jesus himself during his earthly life. The phrase "in accordance with the Scriptures" indicates that Christ's Resurrection fulfilled these predictions.

653 The truth of Jesus' divinity is confirmed by his Resurrection. He had said: "When you have lifted up the Son of man, then you will know that I am he." The Resurrection of the crucified one shows that he was truly "I AM," the Son of God and God himself.

So St. Paul could declare to the Jews: "What God promised to the fathers, this he has fulfilled to us their children by raising Jesus; as also it is written in the second psalm, 'You are my Son, today I have begotten you.'" Christ's Resurrection is closely linked to the Incarnation of God's Son, and is its fulfillment in accordance with God's eternal plan.

654 The Paschal mystery has two aspects: by his death, Christ liberates us from sin; by his Resurrection, he opens for us the way to a new life. This new life is above all justification that reinstates us in God's grace, "so that as Christ was raised from the dead by the glory of the Father, we too might walk in newness of life." Justification consists in both victory over the death caused by sin and a new participation in grace. It brings about filial adoption so that men become Christ's brethren, as Jesus himself called his disciples after his Resurrection: "Go and tell my brethren." We are brethren not by nature, but by the gift of grace, because that adoptive filiation gains us a real share in the life of the only Son, which was fully revealed in his Resurrection.

655 Finally, Christ's Resurrection—and the risen Christ himself—is the principle and source of our future resurrection: "Christ has been raised from the dead, the first fruits of those who have fallen asleep. . . For as in Adam all die, so also in Christ shall all be made alive." The risen Christ lives in the hearts of his faithful while they await that fulfillment. In Christ, Christians "have tasted. . . the powers of the age to come" and their lives are swept up by Christ into the heart of divine life, so that they may "live no longer for themselves but for him who for their sake died and was raised." [29]

Surprised by Hope: Rethinking Heaven, the Resurrection, and the Mission of the Church, N.T. Wright

"The Strange Story of Easter"

There are many smaller arguments which might be brought in at this point, but which we can only summarize. To begin with, the other proposals that are regularly advanced as rival explanations to the early Christian one:

1 Jesus didn't really die; someone gave him a drug which made him look like dead, and he revived in the tomb. Answer: Roman soldiers knew how to kill people, and no disciple would have been fooled by a half-drugged, beat-up Jesus into thinking he'd defeated death and inaugurated the kingdom.

2 When the women went to the tomb they met someone else (perhaps James, Jesus' brother, who looked like him), and in the half-light they thought it was Jesus himself.

Answer: they would have noticed soon enough.

3 Jesus only appeared to people who believed in him. Answer: the accounts make it clear that Thomas and Paul do not come into this category; and actually none of Jesus' followers believed, after his death, that he really was the Messiah, let alone that he was in any sense divine.

4 The accounts we have are biased. Answer: so is all history, all journalism. Every photo is taken by somebody from some angle.

5 They began by saying "he will be raised" as people had done of the martyrs, and this quickly passed into saying "he has been raised" which was functionally equivalent. Answer: no, it wasn't.

6 Lots of people have visions of someone they love who has just died; this was what happened to the disciples. Answer: they knew perfectly well about things like that, and they had language for it; they would say "it's his angel" or "it's his spirit" or "his ghost." They wouldn't say "he's been raised from the dead."

7 Perhaps the most popular: what actually happened was that they had some kind of rich "spiritual" experience, which they interpreted through Jewish categories. Jesus after all really was alive, spiritually, and they were still in touch with him. Answer: that is simply a description of a noble death followed by a Platonic immortality. Resurrection was and is the defeat of death, not simply a nicer description of it; and it's something that happens some while after the moment of death, not immediately.

Equally, we may just notice three of the numerous small-scale arguments which are often, and quite rightly, advanced to support the belief that Jesus did indeed rise from the dead:

1 Jewish tombs, especially those of martyrs, were venerated and often became shrines. There is no sign whatever of that having happened with Jesus' grave.

2 The early church's emphasis on the first day of the week as their special day is very hard to explain unless something striking really did happen then. A gradual or even sudden dawning of faith is hardly sufficient to explain it.

3 The disciples were hardly likely to go out and suffer and die for a belief that wasn't firmly anchored in fact. This is an important point, though subject to the weakness that they might have been genuinely mistaken: they believed the resurrection of Jesus to be a fact, and acted on that belief, but we know (so it would be said) that they were wrong. All this brings us face to face with the ultimate question. The empty tomb and the meetings with Jesus are as well established, by the arguments I have advanced, as any historical data could expect to be. They are, in combination, the only possible explanation for the stories and beliefs that grew up so quickly among Jesus' followers.

How, in turn, do we explain them?

In any other historical enquiry, the answer would be so obvious that it would hardly need saying. Here, of course, this obvious answer ("well, it actually happened") is so shocking, so earth-shattering, that we rightly pause before leaping into the unknown. And here, indeed, as some skeptical friends have cheerfully pointed out to me, it is always possible for anyone to follow the argument so far and to say, simply, "I don't have a good explanation for what happened to cause the empty tomb and the appearances, but I choose to maintain my belief that dead people don't rise and therefore conclude that something else must have happened, even though we can't tell what it was." That is fine; I respect that position; but I simply note that it is indeed then a matter of choice, not a matter of saying that something called "scientific historiography" itself forces us to take that route. [30]

SUGGESTED READING

Wright, N. T. *The Resurrection of the Son of God,* 2003.

27. St. John Chrysostom, "The Easter Sermon of John Chrysostom."
28. Col. 1:13-14 NASB.
29. Catechism of the Catholic Church 651-655: "The Meaning and Saving Significance of the Resurrection", 170-171.
30. Wright, N.T., *Surprised by Hope,* 72-73.

Chapter Seven

Words Are Not Enough

"It is the Holy Spirit, therefore, who instills the sentiment of divine sonship into the heart, who makes us feel (not just know!) that we are children of God. The Spirit himself joins with our spirit to bear witness that we are children of God (Rom. 8:16). This fundamental work of the Holy Spirit sometimes takes places in a sudden and intense way in the life of a person... On the occasion of a retreat ... or on the occasion of prayer for a new releasing of the Spirit the soul is filled with a new light in which God reveals himself in a way as Father. ... A feeling of great trust and confidence and a completely new sense of the condescension of God are experienced. At other times, instead, this revelation of the Father is accompanied by such a strong feeling of God's majesty and transcendence that the soul is overwhelmed." [31]

- Raniero Cantalamessa,
Life in the Lordship of Christ

THE GRACE: *To Be Overwhelmed*

And I will ask the Father, and he will give you another helper [Paraclete], to be with you forever, even the Spirit of truth . . .you know him, for he dwells with you, and will be in you.[32]

John 14:16-17

THEMES

The Holy Spirit...
- Convinces me that Jesus came to rescue me.
- Moves me to surrender.
- Gives me a heart to go rescue others.

---

31. Cantalamessa, *Life in the Lordship of Christ,* 167-168.
32. Jn. 14:16-17 RSV.

QUESTIONS TO CONSIDER

Reflection on the Spirit

- Holy Spirit, help me to know these are not just words.
- Holy Spirit, take me to Calvary.
- Holy Spirit, convince me that Jesus is on the cross for me.
- Holy Spirit, convince me that God is my Father.
- Holy Spirit, convince me that I am his beloved son/ daughter.
- Holy Spirit, overwhelm me now.

_____

_____

_____

_____

_____

_____

_____

_____

Chapter Eight

What Does
He Want from Me?

"...when the Son of Man comes, will he find faith on earth?"

Luke 18:8

THE GRACE: *To Be Overwhelmed*

...God is love.
1 John 4:8

THEMES

What Is Faith?

Faith is *not*:

- *A feeling*
- *Blind*
- *Intellectual assent*

Faith *is*:

- *God's work in me to which I respond*
- *A way of knowing*
- *Surrender*

How Do I Surrender?

- The easier part: *Clinging to the Lord who rescued you*
- The harder, more challenging part: *Detaching from your idols*

QUESTIONS TO CONSIDER

- What are the idols in my life?
- What would detaching from the idols in my life look like practically?

_____

_____

_____

_____

_____

_____

_____

_____

_____

Prayer of Surrender

Father,

I believe that out of your infinite love you created me. I come before you, just as I am, with all my brokenness, wounds, and hurts. I am sorry for all the times I have believed the enemy's lies that you are not a good Father and don't love me. I repent and ask you to forgive me for all of my sins.

Jesus,
Thank you for coming to rescue me from Sin, Death, Hell, and Satan. I surrender to you right now and invite you to be Lord over every area of my entire life.

Come, Holy Spirit,
Flood my soul with the love of the Father and convince me that I matter, I'm worth the trouble, and that in God's eyes I'm worth dying for.

Come, Holy Spirit...

I thirst for you

It is true.

I stand at the door of your heart, day and night. Even when you are not listening, even when you doubt it could be me, I am there: waiting for even the smallest signal of your response, even the smallest suggestion of an invitation that will permit me to enter.

And I want you to know that each time you invite me, I do come always, without fail. Silent and invisible I come, yet with a power and a love most infinite, bringing the many gifts of my Spirit. I come with my mercy, with my desire to forgive and heal you, with a love for you that goes beyond your comprehension—a love every bit as great as the love I have received from the Father. I come, longing to console you and give you strength, to lift you up and bind all your wounds. I bring you my light, to dispel your darkness and all your doubts. I come with my power, that I might carry you and all your burdens; with my grace, to touch your heart and transform your life; and my peace, to still your soul.

I know you like the palm of my hand. I know everything about you. Even the hairs of your head I have counted. Nothing in your life is unimportant to me. I have followed you through the years and I have always loved you even when you have strayed. I know every one of your problems. I know your needs and your worries and yes, I know all your sins.

But I tell you again that I love you, not for what you have or ceased to do, I love you for you, for the beauty and the dignity my Father gave you by creating you in his own image. It is a dignity you have often forgotten, a beauty you have tarnished by sin. But I love you as you are, and I have shed my blood to rescue you. If you only ask me with faith. My grace will touch all that needs changing in your life: I will give you the strength to free yourself from sin and from all its destructive power.

I know what is in your heart; I know your loneliness and all your wounds; the rejections, the judgments, the humiliations. I carried it all before you. And I carried it all for you, so you could share my strength and my victory. I know especially your need for love—how much you are thirsting to be loved and cherished. But how often you have thirsted in vain, by seeking that love selfishly, striving to fill the emptiness inside you with passing pleasures–with even the greater emptiness of sin. Do you thirst for love? "Come to me all who thirst…" (John 7:37). I will satisfy you and fill you. Do you thirst to be loved?

I love you more than you can imagine–to the point of dying on a cross for you.

I thirst for you. Yes, that is the only way to even begin to describe my love for you.

I thirst for you. That is the only way to even begin to describe my love for you. I thirst for you. I thirst to love you and to be loved by you; that is how precious you are to me. I thirst for you. Come to me, and I will fill your heart and heal your wounds. I will make you a new creation and give you peace even in your trials. I thirst for you.

You must never doubt my mercy, my acceptance of you, my desire to forgive, my longing to bless you and live my life in you. I thirst for you. If you feel unimportant in the eyes of the world, that matters not at all. For me, there is no one more important in the world than you. I thirst for you. Open to me, come to me, thirst for me, give me your life, and I will prove to you how important you are for my heart.

Don't you realize that my Father already has a perfect plan to transform your life, beginning from this moment? Trust in me. Ask me every day to enter and take charge of your life, and I will. I promise you before my Father in Heaven that I will work miracles in your life.

Why would I do this? Because I thirst for you. All I ask of you is that you entrust yourself completely to me. I will do all the rest.

Even now, I behold the place my Father has prepared for you in my kingdom. Remember that you are a pilgrim in this life, on a journey home. Sin can never satisfy you, or bring the peace you seek. All that you have sought outside of me has only left you more empty, so do not cling to the things of this life. Above all, do not run from me when you fall. Come to me without delay. When you give me your sins, you give me the joy of being your Savior. There is nothing I cannot forgive and heal; so come now, and unburden your soul.

No matter how far you may wander, no matter how often you forget me, no matter how many crosses you bear in this life; there is one thing I want you to always remember, one thing that will never change: I thirst for you–just as you are. You don't need to change to believe in my love, for it will be your belief in my love that will change you. You forget me, and yet I am seeking you every moment of the day–standing before the doors of your heart and knocking. Do you find this hard to believe?

Then look again at the cross, look at my heart that was pierced for you. Have you not understood my cross? Then listen again to the words I spoke there, for they tell you clearly why I endured all this for you: "I thirst..." *(John 19: 28)*. Yes, I thirst for you. I have never stopped seeking to love you and be loved by you. You have tried many other things in your search for happiness; why not try opening up your heart to me, right now, more than you ever have before? And when you finally open the door of your heart, whenever you come close enough, you will then hear me say to you again and again, not in mere human words but in spirit: No matter what you have done, I love you for your own sake. So come to me with your misery and your sins, with your troubles and needs, and with all your longing to be loved–because I stand at the door of your heart and knock.

Open up to me, for I thirst for you. [33]

- St. Mother Teresa of Calcutta

SUGGESTED READING

Driscoll, Fr. Jeremy. *Awesome Glory: Resurrection in Scripture, Liturgy, and Theology,* 2019.

Driscoll, Fr. Jeremy. *What Happens at Mass,* 2005.

Hahn, Dr. Scott. *The Lamb's Supper: The Mass as Heaven on Earth,* 1999.

---

33. St. Mother Teresa, "I Thirst for You."

Chapter Nine

Getting Clarity on the Mission

"In the high-stakes drama all around us, we have each been given a part to play, one that bears our name and no one else's. We each have the mercy of God to receive, a self to put to death, a Kingdom to gain, a battle to fight and spiritual enemies to slay, comrades to aid, rebels to win over. ... The ancient battle rages all around us, and the adventure we were born for beckons." [34]

- Sophia Consulting,
The Christian Cosmic Narrative

THE GRACE: *Magnanimity*

You are the light of the world ... people [do not] light a lamp and put it under a basket, but on a stand, and it gives light to all in the house.

Matthew 5:14-15

THEMES

The Mission

1. Sabotage and Resistance

_____

_____

_____

_____

_____

_____

2. Reconciliation

_____

_____

_____

_____

_____

_____

3. Re-creation

_____

_____

_____

_____

_____

_____

4. Healing

_____

_____

_____

5. Restoration

_____

_____

_____

_____

_____

6. Ambassadorship

_____

_____

_____

_____

_____

_____

34. Sophia Consulting, _The Christian Cosmic Narrative_, 156.

QUESTIONS TO CONSIDER

- Please read the reflection *"Two other essential missions: Prayer and Suffering"* below. What resonates with me and why?
- Has my understanding of the mission of the disciple changed? How and why?
- Which mission(s) speaks the most to me? Why?

As we conclude this chapter,
prayerfully discern how God may be inviting you
now to write the next chapter of His-story.

_____

_____

_____

_____

_____

_____

_____

Two other essential missions:
Prayer and Suffering

Any attempt to give an exhaustive description of the mission that Jesus sends us in order to accomplish will certainly fall short. In this talk, we have called attention to six missions, if you will, that the Lord calls us to carry out: resistance, reconciliation, re-creation, healing, transformation, and ambassadors.

There are, however, two additional missions that must be mentioned as we close: prayer and suffering.

First, prayer. It is crucial to remember that baptism *really* does something in a person. For example, It really washes away sin; transfers us from the dominion and reign of darkness into the kingdom of God's beloved Son; makes us new creatures; causes us to become temples of the Holy Spirit; incorporates us into the Body of Christ; makes us adopted sons and daughters of God and more besides (cf. Acts 2:38; 22:16; Col. 1:13-14; Rom. 8:14-17;12:4-5; 1 Cor. 6:19; 12:12-14; 2 Cor. 5:17; *The Catechism of the Catholic Church* nos. 1262-1274).

Baptism, though, also makes a person a priest, or, more precisely, to share in Jesus' own priesthood. This is commonly referred to as "the priesthood of all believers," as distinct from the ministerial priesthood. Saint Peter reminds the early Christian community that they are "a chosen race, a royal *priesthood*" (1 Peter 2:5). Peter is talking to all of the people, men and women, who have been reborn in baptism. The seer in Revelation writes, "To him who loves us and has freed us from our sins by his blood and made us a kingdom, priests to his God and Father" (Rev 1:5-6). Likewise, the seer is referring to *everyone* born anew of water and the Holy Spirit.

What do priests *do*? Abbott Jeremy Driscoll says, "It is the priest's work to bring another before God in prayer." We can do this because we have access to God. *This is amazing!* If you tried to walk into the White House to meet the President you would certainly be turned away, and perhaps arrested! If you tried to walk into your doctor's office without an appointment, more than likely you would be told that you have to call and schedule a visit. If you walked in and tried to see the CEO of virtually any organization, you would probably be told it's simply not possible.

But we can talk to God…anytime!

And this is an essential part of our mission as disciples of Jesus. We are all called to stand, sit, kneel, or lie prostrate in agonizing prayer for the world, our spouse, our children, co workers, friends, leaders–everyone and anyone. We are called to lift them up to the One who is Love and desires all men and women to be saved (cf. 1 Tim. 2:4). We are allowed, invited even, to pound on the Sacred Heart of Jesus, the One who has rescued us from Sin, Death, Satan, and Hell.

Priests, however, also offer sacrifices, and this is a second mission we are all sent by Jesus in order to accomplish.

Saint Paul, in his Letter to the Romans, exhorts Christians this way: "Present your bodies as a living sacrifice, holy and acceptable to God, which is your spiritual worship" (Rom. 12:2).

The imagery Paul is drawing on here is rather humorous, even if painful. Sacrifices in his day were usually animals placed by a priest atop an altar to be slain and burned up as an offering to the Roman gods and goddesses. This was done in an attempt to either win the favor of the gods or to appease their wrath. Paul is telling us that we are called to place ourselves on the altar, not to win God's favor or appease him, but out of gratitude for all He has already done for us and so that we can become holy (the literal meaning of sacrifice). A key difference, however, is that we are *living* sacrifices, which means the body keeps crawling off the altar! Each day we have to choose to crawl back on, in gratitude and trusting in our Father's great love made manifest in Jesus.

But is there more to this call to offer ourselves as a sacrifice than meets the eye at first glance?

One of the more challenging verses in all of the Bible is Colossians 1:24. Saint Paul says, "I fill up in my flesh what is lacking in the sufferings of Christ for the sake of his body, which is the Church." What in the world is "lacking" in the sufferings of Christ? Does Paul mean to convey that what Jesus did in going to war to rescue us was close but not quite enough to accomplish all that He came to do? Hardly. The only thing "lacking" in Jesus' suffering is our participation in it.

Now, it must be stated right away, there are two distinct kinds of suffering. On the one hand, there are sufferings we might take on voluntarily, like fasting or some other act of penance; and, on the other hand, there are involuntary sufferings that come to us, like chronic pain or cancer.

As disciples of Jesus we are sent in order to unite our suffering to the cross of Jesus for the sake of the world. This is immensely important since, with regards to involuntary suffering, it's not a question of *if* it's going to come to us in this life, only *how* and *when*.

The narrative of the culture at large sees suffering as a waste, of no value whatsoever. Men and women in nursing homes and hospitals, or confined to their own homes, or wherever pain may find them, can be strongly tempted to think that what they are going through has no point, is of no value, and is in vain.

The disciple of Jesus knows a different story. If we had been there on that day we now call "Good Friday," and seen Jesus on the cross between the two thieves, we would certainly have thought to ourselves, "What an utter waste." We would have thought that nothing good would come from that.

And we would have been wrong.

Disciples of Jesus understand that he rescued us precisely by his suffering on the cross, wherein he revealed to us the Father's love, made atonement for our sins, and went to war to defeat the powers of Sin, Death, and Satan.

Disciples of Jesus likewise understand that Jesus didn't promise us that if we believed in him he would protect us from any and all suffering. Instead, the New Testament is filled with passages on how we will suffer with and for Jesus before we enter fully into his kingdom (cf. among so many verses Mark 8:34; Rom. 8:17; Phil. 1:29; 1 Pet. 4:12-16).

However, as it was with Jesus on the cross, so it is with us when we suffer.

It is not a waste, or in vain, or at least it need not be. When we suffer we can use it. And God can do great things through it.

It was once common to hear someone encourage another who was suffering to "offer it up." That can strike us, perhaps, as being a bit passive. Some have found it more helpful, remembering Paul's words in Col. 1:24, to actively unite what they're going through—chemotherapy, a migraine, chronic back pain, depression, or any other way that suffering comes to us—to the cross of Jesus, trusting that one day they will understand how God used this. The important thing is to understand that nothing we are enduring right now, no matter how painful it may be, need be in vain!

An example of prayer and suffering:

Let me end by offering one final example, one of both prayer and suffering. I mentioned in the video how Jesus used my father as an instrument of healing in my mother's life, so much so that she said to him as he lay in his casket, "Honey, because of you I know who God is." Jesus likewise used my mother as an example of prayer and suffering.

My mom spent most of the last years of her life in intense, chronic pain. Pain is usually measured on a scale of 1-10. Many days her pain was something like a 15. My mother, however, when she was younger, had experienced a miraculous healing, something right out of the pages of the Gospels or The Acts of the Apostles. The point in mentioning that is to say she knew firsthand God's power and that miracles were not confined to the past. She came to understand over time, however, that the same Lord who had once healed her was now inviting her to do the very thing Paul did in his life so many years before: to fill up in her own flesh what was lacking in the sufferings of Christ for the sake of others.

And, so, my mom, without in any way ever romanticizing pain, learned to pray in a new way, learned to crawl atop the altar out of love for the sake of others. When I asked her about this once, she told me that she said to the Lord, "Jesus, you know that I do not want this pain and that I so want you to release me from it. But I trust that this is not in vain, is not useless, is not meaningless—anymore than your cross was. And, so, I unite this to your cross for…" and then she got the idea to start writing down names of people who were in need. At first it was just a few—my dad, her children, her grandchildren and great grandchildren. Over time, however, the lists grew. She started to keep a ledger of prayer intentions on legal pads beside the hospital bed where she lay most of the day, or on the kitchen counter around which she would walk to ease the pain. It might be a couple she heard was having marital difficulties. A young man who was suicidal and battling depression. A girl who was pregnant and considering an abortion. Leaders of nations. People discerning huge decisions. It was overwhelming to see how many names—and how many legal pads!—there were. Gradually, people began to hear about this. They would ask me, or my siblings, to please ask my mom to write their name, or the name of a loved one, in her legal pads.

When my mom finally died and her pain was over, I had an image of Jesus walking with her, taking her on a sort of tour.

As they walked, He started to show her various homes and they were able to look inside the homes and see the people inside. That couple who had been struggling in their marriage and had managed to stay the course. The young man who had persevered through the depression. The young girl and the child she had chosen to keep. On and on they walked together, and after each house,

Jesus simply smiled at my mother and said to her, "It was by my grace that they were able to do those things. But it was your participation in my cross that made it possible. Well done, good and faithful servant!"

To all of you, then, in pain right now, suffering in mind, body, or spirit, please know how valuable, how immensely valuable, you are! You are the spiritual backbone of those who are out there serving as agents of resistance, reconciliation, re-creation, healing, transformation, and ambassadors. Stay strong! Keep the faith! We desperately need you!

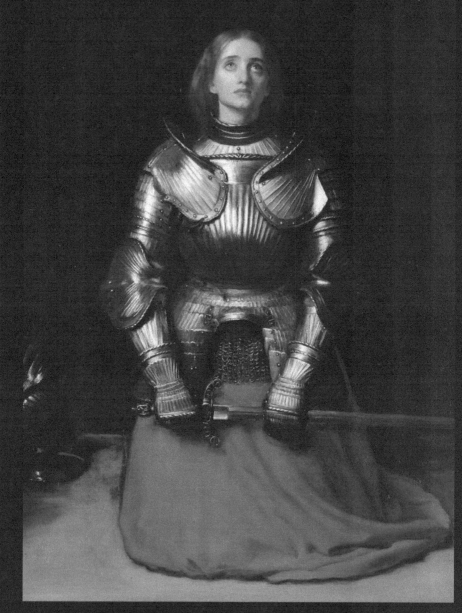

"I am not afraid. God is with me.
I was born for this."
- *St. Joan of Arc*

Know The Story

Rescued People
Rescue People

Bibliography

Baptismal Ritual of the Catholic Church, 158.

Cantalamessa, Raniero. *Life in the Lordship of Christ:* A spiritual commentary on the letter to the Romans. London: Darton, Longman and Todd, 1992.

"The Mystery of Creation"; "The Fall of the Angels"; "Original Sin"; and "The Meaning and Saving Significance of the Resurrection" in the *Catechism of the Catholic Church,* 2nd ed., for the United States of America. Vatican: Libreria Editrice Vaticana, 1994.

The Council of Chalcedon. "The Letter of Pope Leo to Flavian."

Hahn, Dr. Scott. *Commentary on Roman.* Grand Rapids, MI: Baker Academic, a division of Baker Publishing Group, 2017.

Kreeft, Peter. *The Greatest Philosopher Who Ever Lived.* San Francisco, CA: Ignatius Press, 2021.

Knoebel, Thomas L. (quoting Isidore of Seville). "De Ecclesiasticis Officiis, 14.13" in *Sententiae.* Paulist Press, 2008.

Lectionary for Mass. Chicago, IL: Liturgy Training Publications, 2002.

Maximus the Confessor. *Mystery of the Divine Incarnation.*

"The Order of Baptism of Children," English Translation according to the Second Typical Edition. Collegeville, MN: Liturgical Press, 2019.

Ratzinger, Joseph. *Credo for Today: What Christians Believe.* San Francisco, CA: Ignatius Press, 2009.

Sheed, Frank. *To Know Christ Jesus.* San Francisco, CA: Ignatius Press, 2012.

Sophia Consulting. *The Christian Cosmic Narrative, The Deep History of the World*. Detroit, MI: ACTS XXIX Press, 2021.

St. Augustine. "Expositions of the Psalms 51-72 (J.E. Rotelle, Ed.) Vol 17." Hyde Park, New York: New City Press, 2001.

St. Bernard. "The Fountains of the Savior" in *Sermons on Advent & Christmas*. London: Benziger Bros, 1909.

St. Bonaventure. The Soul's Journey to God: The Tree of Life: The Life of St. Francis. Mahwah, NJ: Paulist Press, 1978.

St. Ephrem the Syrian. "A Sermon on the Cross of Christ."

St. Gregory of Nyssa. "Sermon on the Ascension" (chapter XXIV) in *The Great Catechism*.

St. Ignatius of Antioch. "The Second Epistle of Ignatius to the Ephesians, Vol. 1". Buffalo, NY: Christian Literature Company, 1885.

St. Irenaeus. *The Demonstration of the Apostolic Preaching*.

St. John Chrysostom. "The Easter Sermon of John Chrysostom, Pastor of Constantinople."

St. Justin Martyr. "Dialogue with Trypho, (A.D. 155)."

St. Melito of Sardis. "Sermon on The Passover."

St. Mother Teresa of Calcutta. "I Thirst for You."

Wright, N.T. *Surprised by Hope: Rethinking Heaven, the Resurrection, and the Mission of the Church*. HarperOne, an imprint of HarperCollins Publishers, 2018.

Wright, N.T. *Jesus and the Victory of God*. London: SPCK, 2015.